WEATHER

WIND
AND US

Jillian Powell

Illustrated by Cilla Eurich

Belitha Press

First published in Great Britain 1998 by

 Belitha Press Limited
London House, Great Eastern Wharf
Parkgate Road, London SW11 4NQ

Text by Jillian Powell
Illustrations by Cilla Eurich
Text and illustrations copyright © Belitha Press Ltd 1998

Editor Claire Edwards
Series designer Hayley Cove
Picture researcher Diana Morris
Consultants Elizabeth Atkinson and Liz Lewis

ISBN 1 85561 721 8

Printed in Hong Kong

Picture acknowledgements
J.Allan Cash: 14, 16, 20, 28.
Eye Ubiquitous: 18 R.D. Raby.
Getty Images: front cover Peter Cade,
12, 22 Martin Puddy, 24 Randy Wells, 26.
Robert Harding Picture Library: 8 Dr Muller.
Telegraph Colour Library: 4 A.Tilley,
10 Masterfile.
Zefa: 6 Kohlhas.

Contents

Words in **bold** are explained
on pages 30 and 31.

What is the wind?

We can't see the wind, but we can feel it when it blows against our skin or ruffles our hair.

When it blows very hard we can hear it making a whistling sound through windows and under doors.

WIND FACT

Warm air rises above cool air because it is lighter.

Wind blows washing dry by shaking out drops of water. Dampness from the washing disappears into the air.

But what is the wind?

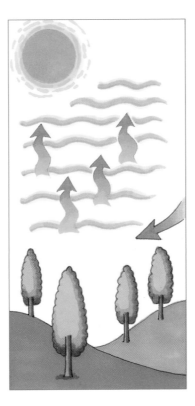

When land is warmed by the sun, the air above it gets warmer too.

The warm air rises and cooler air blows in to take its place.

The moving air is wind.

Windy days

The wind makes clouds race across the sky. It makes patterns of **ripples** on water and in fields of tall grass or crops.

It blows trees about, making their leaves **rustle** and their branches creak.

WIND FACT

A gentle wind is called a **breeze**.

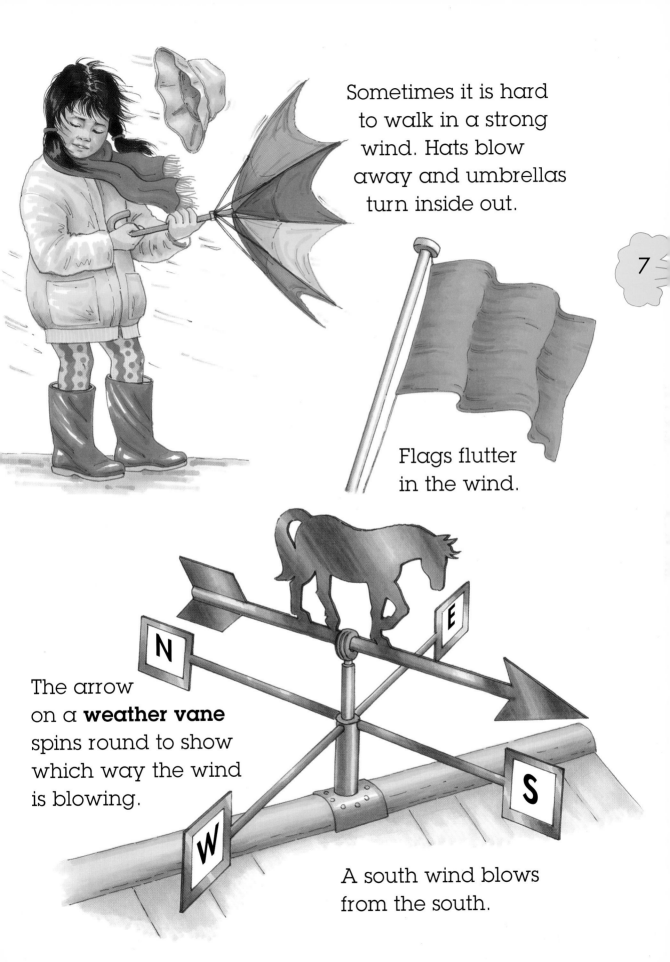

Sometimes it is hard to walk in a strong wind. Hats blow away and umbrellas turn inside out.

Flags flutter in the wind.

The arrow on a **weather vane** spins round to show which way the wind is blowing.

A south wind blows from the south.

Wind power

Have you ever held a pin windmill? The wind makes it spin round and round.

WIND FACT

The wind is a form of **energy** that will never run out.

People have always used the power of wind. Sailors used the wind to blow their ships along.

Windmills were used to grind grain and pump water out of wet land.

The wind turns the **sails** of the windmill to work the machinery inside.

Modern windmills, called wind turbines, are used to make electricity. They are grouped on wind farms in windy places.

Enjoying windy weather

Being outside on a windy day can be exciting and fill us full of **energy**. Fly a kite in an open space and watch how the wind sends it soaring and diving in the sky.

There are lots of other ways to enjoy windy weather.

WIND FACT

Kites were first flown in China about 2500 years ago.

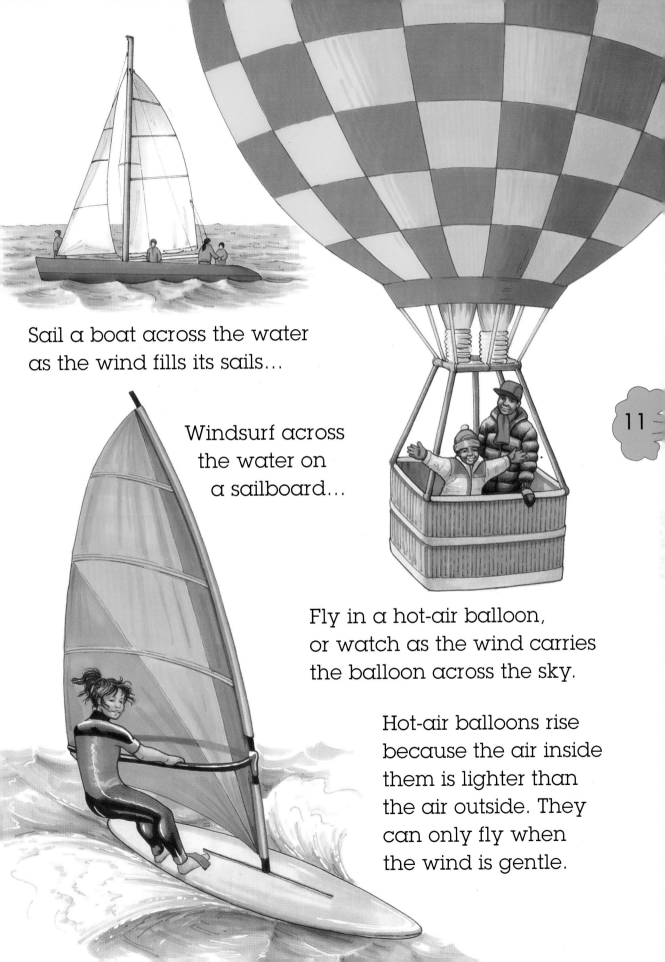

Sail a boat across the water
as the wind fills its sails...

Windsurf across
the water on
a sailboard...

Fly in a hot-air balloon,
or watch as the wind carries
the balloon across the sky.

Hot-air balloons rise
because the air inside
them is lighter than
the air outside. They
can only fly when
the wind is gentle.

Winter and summer winds

Some winds are gentle, others blow hard. Winter winds can blow snow into a **blizzard**. Farm animals can be lost in deep snow.

Snowstorms make it difficult to see, so driving is dangerous. The wind can pile snow into deep **snowdrifts**.

WIND FACT

Wind that blows very hard can burn your skin.

12

The wind makes a cold day feel colder. We call this **wind chill**. Clothes keep out the wind and trap warm air around the body.

13

Summer **breezes** may cool hot sunny days. At the seaside, people sometimes sit behind **wind breaks** if the breeze is strong.

Wind, plants and animals

The wind spreads the seeds of plants and trees. The seeds are very light so they can be carried a long way. The puffball mushroom puffs out clouds of **spores** when the wind blows against it.

WIND FACT

Dandelion seeds can be carried up to 10 kilometres by the wind.

Some seeds have wings that act like tiny helicopters. Others float like **parachutes**.

A bird's feathers help it glide in the wind. Steady winds help **migrating** birds to fly thousands of kilometres.

Rabbits sniff the air while they are feeding. The wind can carry the **scent** of a **predator**, and warn the rabbits that danger is near.

Stormy winds

In stormy weather, the wind blows very hard and heavy rain falls. Trees can be blown down, crushing cars and blocking roads. **Power lines** can be broken, leaving homes without heat and light.

WIND FACT

The strongest wind in the world is called a **hurricane**.

Stormy winds blow chimneys and roof tiles off houses.

Tornadoes are the fastest winds in the world. They spin and swirl over land at more than 300 kilometres per hour.

Gales blow the sea into huge waves that can flood the land. Ferries and fishing boats have to stay in a **harbour**.

17

Measuring the wind

Weather forecasters take information about the wind from **weather balloons**, and from ships and aircraft.

They use the information to make weather maps and **weather forecasts**. This instrument is an anemometer. The top spins round to show how fast the wind is blowing.

WIND FACT

Wind blows rain clouds round the world and brings our weather.

Satellites fly round the earth and collect information about the weather.
They send pictures back to earth.

On a weather map, this sign 🔄(16) shows that the wind is blowing from the south at 16 kilometres per hour.

Sailors, farmers and aircraft pilots all use weather forecasts.

They need to know when it is going to be windy. **Windsocks** at airports and sea ports show which way and how fast the wind is blowing.

Staying safe in the wind

Tall buildings like skyscrapers are built from strong materials, such as concrete and steel, so they are not damaged when winds howl round them.

WIND FACT

Sometimes bridges have to be closed when the wind is very strong.

People build
sea walls to stop the
wind blowing waves
on to the land and
causing floods.

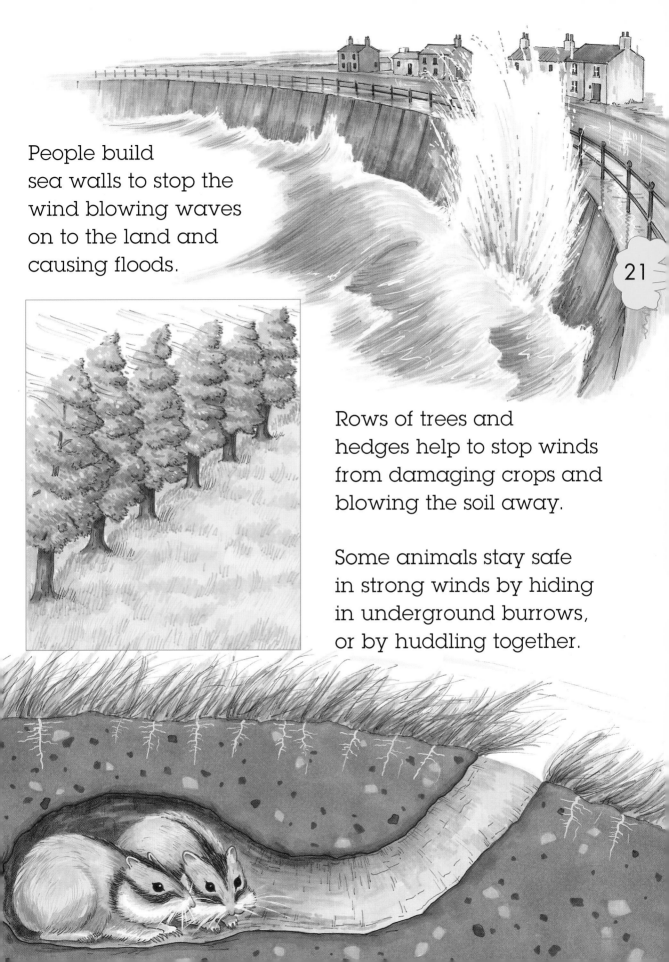

Rows of trees and
hedges help to stop winds
from damaging crops and
blowing the soil away.

Some animals stay safe
in strong winds by hiding
in underground burrows,
or by huddling together.

Winds around the world

In some parts of the world there are winds called monsoons. For part of the year they blow from the land.

Then they change direction and blow from the sea, bringing heavy rain. This city in India has been flooded by monsoon rains.

WIND FACT

Chinook means snow-eater in a local language.

Some winds have special names.

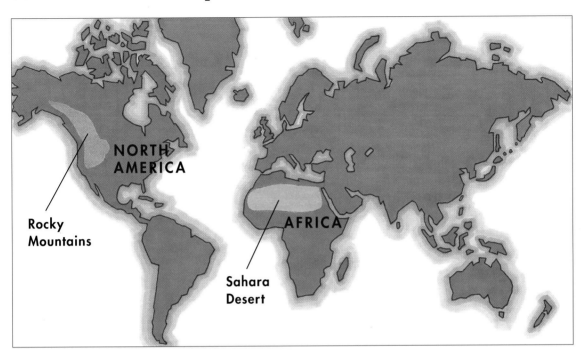

The chinook is a warm, dry wind that blows across the Rocky Mountains in North America. It can melt snow in a few hours.

The sirocco is a hot, dusty wind that blows off the Sahara **Desert** in North Africa.

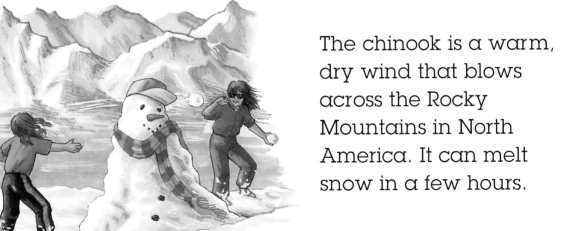

Shaping the land

Wind can shape the way things look. In the **desert** it makes patterns of **ripples** in the sand, and blows it into high **dunes**.

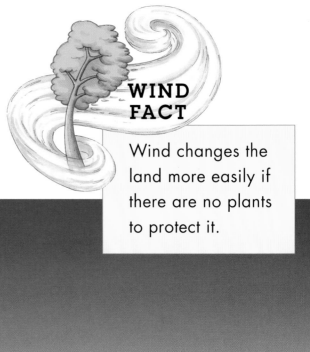

WIND FACT

Wind changes the land more easily if there are no plants to protect it.

24

Plants that grow in very windy places stay short. They spread out their roots and grow close together to keep out of the wind.

Wind blows rain or bits of sand against rocks. Over a long time this can **wear** the rocks into strange shapes.

When winds always blow the same way, they can make trees twist and bend over as they grow.

Harmful winds

Fire and smoke are carried by the wind. After hot, dry weather wind can spread forest fires by blowing sparks and flames through the dry wood.

WIND FACT

Wide forest paths help to stop fires from spreading.

Fumes from cars, factories and power stations cause air **pollution**.

The pollution in the air turns clean rain into **acid rain**.

Acid rain kills trees and makes lakes poisonous. It also eats away the stone on buildings.

The wind can blow pollution from one country to make acid rain in another country.

Wind worship

Strong winds can be powerful and dangerous. People have always been afraid of them.

People once believed the winds were gods and built **temples** to them. The Temple of the Winds in **Athens** was built about 2000 years ago. When it was first built it had a **weather vane** on top, one of the first in the world.

WIND FACT

In Chinese **myths**, Mrs Wind rode among the clouds on a tiger.

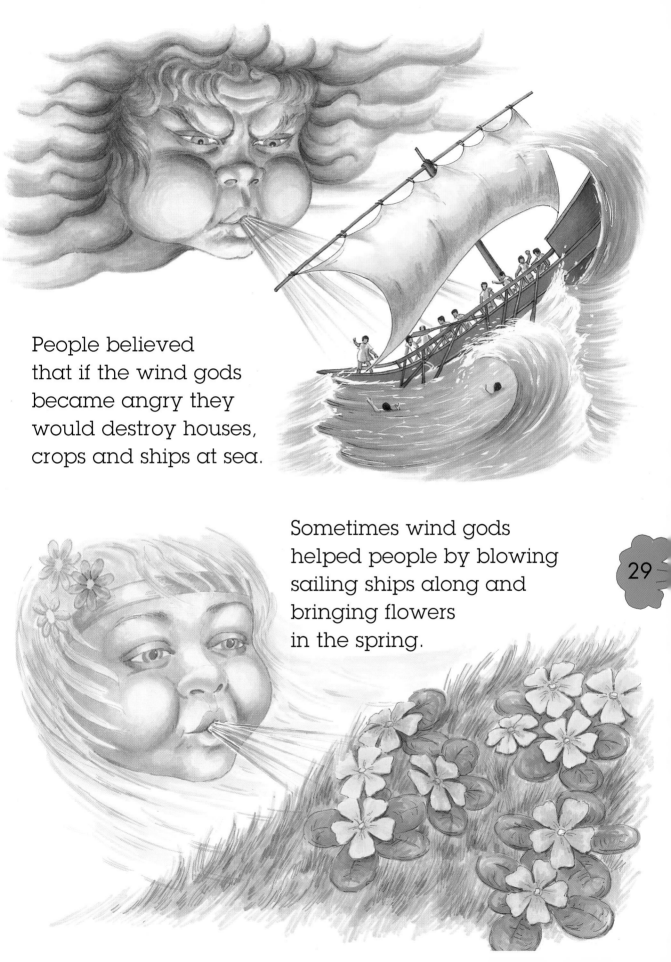

People believed
that if the wind gods
became angry they
would destroy houses,
crops and ships at sea.

Sometimes wind gods
helped people by blowing
sailing ships along and
bringing flowers
in the spring.

Words to remember

acid rain Rain that carries pollution.

Athens The capital city of Greece.

blizzard A snowstorm where the wind blows the snow very hard.

breeze A light wind.

desert A hot, dry place where there is little or no rain.

dune Sand piled into heaps by the wind.

energy Power to make things move. Energy gives us strength to do things.

fumes Poisonous smoke.

gale A very strong wind.

harbour Sheltered water where boats are kept.

hurricane A strong wind that spins round and round. A hurricane begins at sea.

migrating Travelling from one place to another.

myth A story made up to explain why things in the world are the way they are.

parachute A large piece of material that people use to help them fall slowly and safely from an aeroplane.

pollution Dirt made by people and machines that harms the earth.

power lines Wires that carry electricity to people's homes.

predator An animal that eats other animals.

ripples Small wave-like movements.

rustle A quiet sound, like the sound you make when you walk through dry leaves.

sails The arms of a windmill are called sails or vanes.

satellite A special spacecraft that flies round the earth. It collects information and sends it to computers on earth as numbers or photographs.

scent Another word for smell, often used about animals.

snowdrifts Snow piled up by the wind.

spores The seeds of some plants, such as mushrooms.

temple A place where people pray and worship.

tornado a strong wind that spins round and round. A tornado begins on land.

wear To rub away, or erode.

weather balloons Balloons carrying equipment that tells us about the weather.

weather forecast A report that tells us what the weather will be like in the future.

weather vane A machine that shows which way the wind is blowing.

wind break Anything that shelters people or plants from the wind.

wind chill When the wind makes the air colder.

windsock A piece of cloth like a large sock that fills with wind and shows which way and how fast the wind is blowing. The foot end points away from the wind. The stronger the wind, the higher the end rises.

Index

32